GEORGIA

Past and Present

Stephanie Watson

rosen publishing's
rosen
central®

New York

Published in 2010 by The Rosen Publishing Group, Inc.
29 East 21st Street, New York, NY 10010

Copyright © 2010 by The Rosen Publishing Group, Inc.

First Edition

All rights reserved. No part of this book may be reproduced in any form without permission in writing from the publisher, except by a reviewer.

Library of Congress Cataloging-in-Publication Data

Watson, Stephanie, 1969–
Georgia: past and present / Stephanie Watson.—1st ed.
    p. cm.—(The United States: past and present)
Includes bibliographical references and index.
ISBN-13: 978-1-4358-5292-1 (library binding)
ISBN-13: 978-1-4358-5582-3 (pbk)
ISBN-13: 978-1-4358-5583-0 (6 pack)
1. Georgia—Juvenile literature. I. Title.
F286.3.W38 2010
975.8—dc22

2008054225

Manufactured in the United States of America

On the cover: Top left: The Battle of Chickamauga, fought between the Confederate and Union armies on September 18–20, 1863, was one of the deadliest battles of the Civil War. Top right: The gold dome of the capitol building in Atlanta sparkles in the Georgia sun. Bottom: The Okefenokee Swamp is the largest swamp in North America.

Contents

Introduction   5

Chapter 1
The Land of Georgia   6

Chapter 2
The History of Georgia   12

Chapter 3
The Government of Georgia   20

Chapter 4
The Economy of Georgia   26

Chapter 5
People from Georgia:
Past and Present   32

Timeline   38

Georgia at a Glance   39

Glossary   41

For More Information   42

For Further Reading   44

Bibliography   45

Index   46

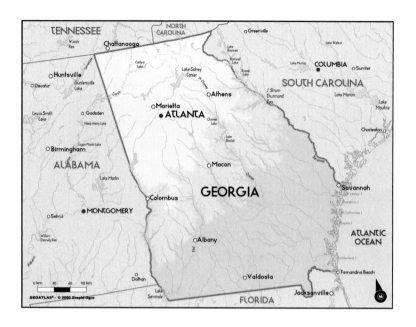

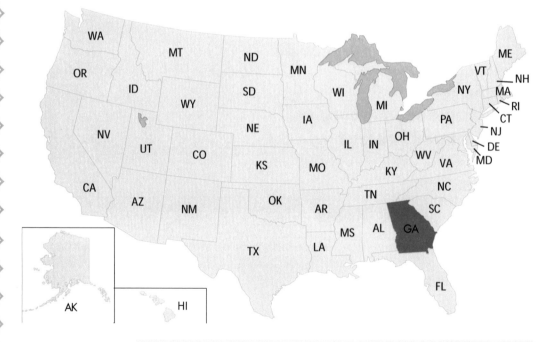

Georgia is located in the southeastern United States, bordered by North Carolina, South Carolina, the Atlantic Ocean, Florida, Alabama, and Tennessee.

Introduction

In 1733, a group of colonists from England arrived in the area of Savannah, Georgia. They were impressed by its geography and climate. The landscape was lush and green, and the weather seemed perfectly suited to growing crops. They named their new colony Georgia, in honor of King George II of England.

Today, Georgia looks much different from the way it did when the English colonists first settled there. Where once there were small farms and villages, now there are big cities with tall skyscrapers. What started as a small colony of just 120 people has grown into a state of nearly 10 million people.

Georgia has become a center of agriculture and industry. Many of the country's biggest corporations, from Coca-Cola to Delta Air Lines, have offices and factories in the state. Georgia is home to the world's busiest airport, Hartsfield-Jackson Atlanta International Airport, and it is the biggest U.S. producer of peanuts, pecans, and poultry.

Georgia has also been home to some of the world's greatest artists, musicians, writers, businesspeople, and politicians. Ray Charles, James Brown, Alice Walker, and former president Jimmy Carter have all lived in—and left their mark on—the state.

Although Georgia has grown and become modern, its history is still alive today. The people of Georgia won't soon forget that their state was one of the original thirteen colonies. Georgia was a center in the Civil War and in the civil rights movement.

Chapter 1

THE LAND OF GEORGIA

On a map of the United States, Georgia is located just above Florida in the southeastern part of the country. Its other neighbors are Tennessee and North Carolina to the north, South Carolina to the northeast, and Alabama to the west. The Atlantic Ocean lies along Georgia's southeastern coast.

Georgia measures 57,906 square miles (149,976 square kilometers) in total area. Although it is only the twenty-fourth-largest state in the country, it is the second-largest in the Southeast. The exact center of Georgia is found in Twiggs County, about 20 miles (32 km) southeast of Macon.

Georgia's Five Regions

Georgia has five distinct geographic areas: the Appalachian Plateau, Appalachian Ridge and Valley, Blue Ridge, Piedmont Plateau, and Atlantic Coastal Plain.

The Appalachian Plateau is a mountainous region that stretches all the way from the state of New York to the northern parts of Georgia and Alabama. It extends into a tiny piece of Georgia's northwest corner. The plateau is about 1,800 to 2,000 feet (549 to 610 meters) above sea level. Sand Mountain is located on the eastern side of the plateau, and Lookout Mountain straddles Tennessee and Georgia. At the top of Lookout Mountain is an attraction called Rock City, where one can view seven states: Georgia, Tennessee, Alabama, North Carolina, South Carolina, Virginia, and Kentucky.

The Appalachian Ridge and Valley region takes up a big section of northwest Georgia. It's made up of long narrow sandstone ridges with low U-shaped valleys in between. Forests cover most of the ridges, whereas the valleys are mainly farmland. The Ridge and Valley region includes the Great Valley, Chickamauga Valley, and Armuchee Ridges.

From the top of Lookout Mountain, visitors can get a spectacular view of seven U.S. states.

The Blue Ridge region takes up the northeast corner of Georgia. It is made up of mountains (mainly the Blue Ridge Mountains), ridges, and bowl-shaped areas called basins. Georgia's highest mountains are in this area, including Brasstown Bald, which, at 4,784 feet (1,458 m) above sea level, is Georgia's tallest peak.

Georgia Coastline

Sixty million years ago, if someone had tried to visit what is now the Georgia coastline, that person would have been deep underwater. Way back then, Georgia's coastline ran through what is today the area that contains Augusta and Macon in the center of the state. That ancient coastline is now the fall line that separates the Coastal Plain from the Piedmont Plateau region.

During the Pleistocene epoch, which began about two million years ago, the polar ice caps repeatedly froze and thawed. As they froze, sea levels dropped. As they melted, sea levels rose. Over time, this rise and fall of water helped form the modern Georgia coast. Winds, waves, currents, and tides created the Barrier Islands off the coasts of Georgia, South Carolina, and Florida. Today, the Georgia coast and Barrier Islands are favorite vacation spots for people from all over the country and the world.

The Piedmont Plateau gets its name from the French word *piedmont*, which means "foot of the mountain." The plateau does lie at the foot of the Blue Ridge Mountains, and it slopes gently down to the Coastal Plain. Its rolling hills and valleys provide some of the most fertile farmland in Georgia. Much of the soil in this area is the well-known Georgia red clay.

The Atlantic Coastal Plain is Georgia's largest region. Between the Piedmont Plateau and Coastal Plain regions is a 20-mile-wide (32 km) border called the fall line. From there, the elevation drops from about 800 feet (244 m) to sea level at the coast. The Upper Coastal Plain is hilly and good for farming, while the Lower Coastal Plain is a flat area made up of marshes, swamps, and wetlands.

Off the coast is a string of about one hundred islands. They are called the Barrier Islands because they form a barrier between the ocean and land, protecting the mainland from the effects of wind, waves, and tides. The major Barrier Islands are Cumberland, Jekyll, St. Simons, and Tybee.

Rivers, Lakes, and Swamps

For a state that is mostly landlocked, Georgia has a lot of water. In addition to the 100 miles (160 km) of coastline along the Atlantic Ocean, the state has 70,000 miles (113,000 km) of rivers and streams, and several major lakes.

The sun rises over the Chattahoochee River, which is an important source of both drinking water and recreation.

Most of the rivers in Georgia are used for hydroelectric power, water supply, fishing, and recreation. The state's three major rivers are the following:

The Chattahoochee River, which runs 436 miles (702 km) from northern Georgia into Alabama. This river supplies most of Atlanta's drinking water—about 300 million gallons (1.1 billion liters) per day.

The Savannah River, which is 350 miles (563 km) in length. It borders Georgia and South Carolina.

The Suwannee River, which starts at the Okefenokee Swamp in southern Georgia and flows 266 miles (428 km) into Florida. Composer Stephen Foster wrote the song "Old Folks at Home" in 1851 about

Sandhill cranes take flight at the Okefenokee National Wildlife Refuge. Sandhill cranes and wood ducks live peacefully in the Okefenokee Swamp all year round.

being down on the Suwannee River (the song is also known as "Swanee River"), and it became very popular.

When the land of Georgia formed millions of years ago, there weren't many natural lakes. People decided to make their own lakes by building dams in rivers or stream valleys and causing the water to flood and collect in a reservoir. Today, there are several major lakes in Georgia, including Lake Lanier, Lake Hartwell, Clarks Hill Lake, and Lake Seminole. Many people own homes along the lakes, and they go there in droves each summer to boat, fish, and swim.

Georgia is also home to natural wetlands known as swamps. Although the word may make them sound like mysterious places inhabited by strange creatures, swamps are actually beautiful wetlands filled with wildlife. The biggest swamp in the country—the Okefenokee—is in Georgia. Its name means "land of the trembling earth." If a person walks in the Okefenokee Swamp, the earth will tremble. The swamp is not solid ground but is instead covered in floating mats of peat. It is contained within the Okefenokee National Wildlife Refuge, which is home to one of the largest alligator populations in the world. It's also home to hundreds of other animals, including more than two hundred kinds of birds and more than sixty types of reptiles.

Chapter 2

THE HISTORY OF GEORGIA

About ten thousand years ago, Native Americans inhabited the area that is now Georgia. Most of them were the Creek and Cherokee peoples. They lived in villages, where they farmed and hunted.

In the 1500s, Spanish ships began to land along the coasts of what are now Georgia and South Carolina. Spanish general Hernando de Soto came with his army in search of gold. Though there was gold in Georgia, de Soto and his soldiers never found it.

They didn't strike it rich, but the Spanish liked Georgia enough to stay. They claimed it and its neighbor Florida for Spain.

England also took notice of the warm climate and fertile soil in the southeastern part of North America. In 1607, England established its first permanent North American colony in Jamestown, Virginia. The English colonists began pushing southward and challenging the Spanish for control of the southern colonies.

James Edward Oglethorpe and the New British Colony

England was prosperous in the 1700s, but not every citizen there was doing well. Many people were poor. Those who could not afford to pay their debts were put in prisons. A member of England's Parliament, James Edward Oglethorpe, felt sorry for these prisoners and wanted to help set up a place where they could be free and earn a good living. In 1730, he sent a petition to King George II asking for a piece of land in North America where the debtors could live. The land would also act as a buffer, protecting English settlements in South Carolina against the Spanish in Florida.

James Oglethorpe (1696–1785), a member of the Parliament, planned a colony in America where England's debtors could make a new beginning.

On June 9, 1732, King George II granted a charter for the new colony, which would occupy the land between the Savannah and Altamaha rivers. It was named Georgia in the king's honor. Oglethorpe and a group called the Trustees for Establishing the Colony of Georgia in America were put in charge of the new colony. The trustees were given control of Georgia for twenty-one years.

The first boatload of 120 English colonists arrived at Yamacraw Bluff (now Savannah, Georgia) on February 12, 1733. Each colonist had enough food and supplies to last one year. They were given tools, seeds, and a plot of land on which to live and farm.

Oglethorpe worked hard to build his colony. He oversaw the design and building of Savannah. He and the colonists planted mulberry trees on which to breed silkworms. Oglethorpe also helped secure Georgia for England. In July 1742, he and his troops fought the Spanish in the Battle of Bloody Marsh on St. Simons Island. Oglethorpe and one thousand soldiers battled five thousand Spanish soldiers, yet the outnumbered English troops won the battle and drove the Spanish out of Georgia forever.

Over time, the colonists discovered that Georgia wasn't all they had hoped it would be. The summers were very hot, with violent storms. Silkworms didn't want to eat the type of mulberry trees that were growing in Georgia. In 1752, feeling that their new colony could not succeed, the trustees turned Georgia over to the government of England. Georgia became a royal colony. Oglethorpe went back to England and never returned to Georgia.

From Independence to Revolution

By the 1770s, the demand for independence from England began to echo throughout the thirteen colonies in America. Georgians were split on the idea. About half wanted to remain a royal colony, while the other half wanted independence. Eventually, the independence-minded patriots got their way.

In 1776, three Georgia representatives—George Walton, Lyman Hall, and Button Gwinnett—went to Philadelphia to sign the Declaration of Independence. Georgians fought courageously in the American Revolution. In 1781, English troops surrendered at Yorktown in Virginia, putting an end to the fighting. With the signing of the Treaty of Paris in 1783, the American Revolution was officially over. On January 2, 1788, Georgia voted to ratify (approve) the U.S. Constitution, becoming the fourth state in the nation.

In 1838, the U.S. government forced the Cherokees to leave their homes in Georgia and walk westward to present-day Oklahoma. The Cherokee march became known as the Trail of Tears.

The Trail of Tears

Native Americans had been the first residents of Georgia, and by the early 1800s, their societies were very advanced. The Cherokees had their own constitution, newspaper, and system of writing. Yet many white Americans still considered the Native Americans to be savages and wanted them out of the southeastern United States. In 1830, U.S. president Andrew Jackson signed the Indian Removal Act. This act forced Native Americans to leave their homes and move to the land that is today Oklahoma in the western part of the country.

The Georgia Flag

The first Georgia flag was raised in Savannah on November 8, 1860. It was a secession flag, flown by the states that wanted to remove themselves from the Union. It read, "Our Motto, Southern States, Equality of the States, Don't Tread on Me."

On October 17, 1879, after the Civil War, the first official Georgia state flag was adopted. It had one vertical blue bar on the left side and three horizontal bands of red, white, and red.

The flag changed several times over the years. In 1956, it contained the Confederate battle flag, which had a red background with a large blue "X" lined with white stripes in the center. Some Georgians saw the Confederate flag as a sign of their heritage, yet others felt it was a symbol of racism because the Confederates had been in favor of slavery. Georgia lawmakers and residents argued over the flag for many years. In 2003, Georgia adopted a new state flag. This flag, which still flies today, has red and white stripes with the state seal in the upper-left corner.

In 1838, the U.S. Army rounded up more than fifteen thousand Cherokees and forced them to march west. Nearly four thousand died of disease, starvation, or exposure to the elements during the 800-mile (1,287 km) walk, known as the Trail of Tears.

Secession and the Civil War

Although Georgia's early founders did not allow slavery at first, over time slaves were brought to the colony to help with agriculture. By 1861, the state had about 460,000 slaves—among the highest slave populations in the nation. The Northern states and newly elected president Abraham Lincoln wanted to end slavery. Georgia plantation owners refused to give up the practice.

On January 19, 1861, Georgia voted to secede from the Union of Northern states. It joined the Confederate States of America (CSA), along with ten other Southern states that were pro-slavery. The CSA had its own constitution, president (Jefferson Davis, a former U.S. secretary of war), vice president (Alexander Hamilton Stephens, a former U.S. congressman and a slaveholder from Georgia), and army.

In April 1861, the Confederacy captured Fort Sumter in South Carolina, starting the Civil War. One of the bloodiest battles was fought in Georgia. In September 1863, troops fought for two days at the Battle of Chickamauga in north Georgia. The Confederate soldiers, under the command of General Braxton Bragg, forced General William S. Rosecrans and the Union troops to retreat to Chattanooga, Tennessee. More than eighteen thousand Confederate soldiers and sixteen thousand Union soldiers died.

By 1864, Union soldiers had gained ground. On May 5, Union general William Tecumseh Sherman and 100,000 of his troops began marching from Chattanooga, Tennessee, to Georgia. They reached Atlanta on September 2, 1864, and began setting every structure on fire. The fire spread quickly. Out of 3,800 buildings in the city, only about 400 remained after the Union troops were finished.

General Sherman's March to the Sea left a 60-mile-wide (100 km), 300-mile-long (500 km) path of destruction from Atlanta to Savannah. The Union army either took or destroyed almost everything in their path. On December 21, 1864, Savannah fell to the Union troops. By the time the Confederate army surrendered to the Union army in April 1865, forty thousand of Georgia's residents had either been killed in the war or had left the state.

In 1864, near the end of the Civil War, General William Tecumseh Sherman and his Union troops burned Atlanta and other Georgia cities to the ground during their March to the Sea.

Martin Luther King Jr. and the Civil Rights Movement

After the Civil War, the slaves were freed and Georgia began a new era. Unfortunately, life remained difficult for African Americans living in the state. Many of Georgia's white residents were not content to live side by side with its black residents. In the late 1800s and early 1900s, more than 450 African Americans were lynched (killed without cause). The Ku Klux Klan, a secret racist organization, grew in members.

Throughout the South, black people were segregated because of their race. They could not attend the same schools, eat at the same restaurants, or even use the same bathrooms as white people. This system of segregation was called Jim Crow—named after a black character portrayed by white performers in the 1830s. It was a cruel and humiliating system based on discrimination and inequality.

A few brave African Americans stood up against segregation. On December 1, 1955, seamstress Rosa Parks was arrested when she refused to give up her seat to a white passenger on a Montgomery, Alabama, bus. Reverend Martin Luther King Jr., who was born in Atlanta and was a pastor in Montgomery at the time, organized a bus boycott to protest Parks's arrest. King

Rosa Parks's refusal to give her bus seat to a white rider in Montgomery, Alabama, in 1955 helped start the civil rights movement.

led nonviolent protests called sit-ins throughout the South. He rose to become the leader of the civil rights movement.

Over time, King's efforts led to many hard-won achievements. In 1961, the University of Georgia in Athens admitted its first black students. In 1964, the U.S. Congress passed the Civil Rights Act. This act banned segregation and provided equal rights for all Americans, regardless of their race, color, religion, sex, or national origin.

Chapter 3
THE GOVERNMENT OF GEORGIA

After the United States declared its independence from England in 1776, Georgia adopted its own government and constitution. The Georgia General Assembly was established by the state constitution in 1777—twelve years before the U.S. Congress was created. At first, the General Assembly consisted of only one house. In 1789, it was split into a House of Representatives and a Senate, which is the way it remains today.

The Georgia Constitution

The most important document in the state of Georgia is its constitution, which forms the framework of the state's government. It has authority over any law passed in Georgia.

Georgia has had ten different constitutions over the years. The first was signed in 1777. The final revision, which became effective in 1983, is the one used today. If the Georgia government wants to change (amend) the constitution again, it needs two-thirds of both the Georgia House of Representatives and Senate to vote in favor of the change. Then, Georgia residents must vote on the amendment during a general election.

Branches of Georgia's Government

The Georgia government is made up of three branches: the executive, the legislative, and the judicial branches. Each branch has a unique role in governing the state.

Executive branch This is the largest branch of Georgia's government. At the top of the executive branch is the governor, who is an elected official. To be governor of Georgia, a person must be at least thirty years old and have been a U.S. citizen for fifteen years and a Georgia resident for six years. The governor serves a four-year term and can be reelected for one additional four-year term.

The Georgia constitution, first signed in 1777, established the state government. Pictured here is page two from the 1789 version of the state's constitution.

The governor's office is in the gold-domed state capitol building in downtown Atlanta. The role of the governor includes proposing new bills and carrying out new laws when they are enacted, setting the state budget, appointing members of state government boards, and vetoing bills passed by the Georgia legislature if he or she doesn't

The state capitol building in Atlanta is the center of Georgia's government. Much of the building was constructed from Georgia marble and was completed in 1889.

agree with those bills. Other elected officials in the executive branch include the lieutenant governor, secretary of state, attorney general, and superintendent of schools.

Legislative branch The legislative branch is known as the Georgia General Assembly. It is made up of two branches: the House of Representatives and the Senate. With 180 members in the House of Representatives and 56 members in the Senate, the Georgia General Assembly is one of the largest state legislatures in the nation. Both senators and representatives are elected to serve two-year terms.

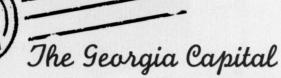

The Georgia Capital

Between 1777 and today, the state capital changed locations more than a dozen times.

1777–1778	Savannah	Georgia's revolutionary government made Savannah its first state capital.
1779–1780	Augusta	When the English captured Savannah, the government was forced to move to Augusta.
1780–1781	Heard's Fort	After Augusta fell to the English, the capital was temporarily moved to Heard's Fort in Wilkes County.
1781–1782	Augusta	The government returned to Augusta.
1782	Savannah	When the English evacuated Savannah, the Georgia government moved back into the city.
1783–1785	Augusta and Savannah	For three years, the General Assembly went back and forth four times between Augusta and Savannah.
1786–1796	Augusta	Augusta became the second official state capital.
1796–1806	Louisville	The third official state capital was named after King Louis XVI of France.
1807–1868	Milledgeville	The Georgia legislature voted to move the capital closer to the geographic middle of the state. Milledgeville was named after John Milledge, the Georgia governor from 1802 to 1806.
1868–present	Atlanta	After the Civil War, Atlanta became the state capital.

Members of the Georgia state senate work to pass legislation. Two chambers make up the Georgia General Assembly: the Senate and the House of Representatives.

Both the House and Senate pass new laws, consider changes to the Georgia constitution, and help write the budget. For a law to be passed, members of both the House and Senate must agree on it, and then the governor must sign it into law.

Judicial branch This branch is in charge of interpreting and enforcing state laws. It contains three different levels of courts: superior courts, the court of appeals, and the Georgia Supreme Court. Superior courts try criminal cases (which involve a violation of the law) and civil cases (which are related to legal issues that are noncriminal, such as a lawsuit against a company), usually with the

24

help of a jury. The court of appeals has twelve judges who hear appeals from defendants who lost their cases in superior courts. All judges are elected. The supreme court is the highest court in Georgia. It consists of seven justices who hear any appeal that has to do with the U.S. Constitution or Georgia constitution. Judges on the supreme court and court of appeals serve for six years.

Local Governments

Georgia's three main branches of government handle all the big-picture issues, such as passing and enforcing laws. Local governments handle all the everyday work, from building roads to providing public education for all Georgia's students.

Georgia has 159 counties, which are in charge of elections, roads, health, and automobile licenses. They also handle police and fire departments, recreational facilities, and public housing. Counties are usually run by a board of commissioners. Most commissioners are elected to serve four-year terms, but in some counties, they may serve for as many as six years. Within the counties are cities, each of which is run by a mayor and city council. There are special districts, which operate public schools, airports, and public transportation.

THE ECONOMY OF GEORGIA

Chapter 4

In the early days of Georgia's history, cotton was the state's major product. Although cotton is still a chief crop there, Georgia ranks first in U.S. peanut production today. Peaches are also an important crop to the state, and it currently ranks third in U.S. peach production. Georgia is sometimes nicknamed "the Peach State." Agriculture is a vital part of the local economy, but Georgia is also home to a thriving business community. Many of the world's biggest companies, including CNN, the United Parcel Service (UPS), and the insurance company AFLAC, are headquartered in the state of Georgia.

Georgia's total value of goods and services produced (gross domestic product, or GDP) was more than $396 billion in 2007. Approximately 4.2 million people have jobs in the state.

Getting Around: Georgia Transportation

Part of the reason for Georgia's economic success is its vast transportation network. Companies can easily transport their goods throughout the state and to other parts of the country—and world— by way of Georgia's roadways, railways, airports, and harbors.

Planes Hartsfield-Jackson Atlanta International Airport is the busiest airport in the world. More than eighty-nine million

Hartsfield-Jackson Atlanta International Airport is the busiest airport in the world, even busier than Chicago's O'Hare International Airport.

passengers move through its 5.8-million-square-foot (539,000 square meter) terminal each year. Georgia also has 472 other public and private airports serving travelers and businesses.

Georgia is the home of Delta Air Lines, which started in 1924 as a crop-dusting service to combat the boll weevils that were destroying the cotton crops. Today, it is the world's largest airline, offering service to more than 500 destinations in more than 105 countries.

Trains In 1833, as the railway business was booming across the United States, the first railroad tracks were laid in Georgia. By 1860, train tracks crisscrossed the entire state. The Western and Atlantic

Georgia Agriculture

In the 1800s, cotton was Georgia's main crop. By the mid-1820s, plantations were producing 150,000 bales of it per year—more cotton than was produced in any other place in the world. Eli Whitney's cotton gin made harvesting the crop less costly and more efficient. Plantation owners became wealthy and powerful.

In 1915, a swarm of beetle-like insects called boll weevils arrived in Georgia from Mexico. They ate their way through nearly 3.5 million acres of cotton crops, destroying the state's major industry. Today, cotton has come back in Georgia, but it is no longer the state's largest crop. Peanuts, pecans, eggs, poultry, and rye are now Georgia's most plentiful agricultural products.

This farmer near Pitts, Georgia, holds a cluster of peanuts. The peanut is one of the state's biggest food exports.

Railroad was Georgia's main railroad, connecting the state to Tennessee. Georgia now has nearly 5,000 miles (8,046 km) of railroads. CSX and Norfolk-Southern are the major freight railroads, carrying goods in and out of the state. The Metropolitan Atlanta Rapid Transit Authority (MARTA) provides public transportation, and Amtrak carries passengers from Georgia to the rest of the country.

Automobiles Anyone who has a car can travel anywhere in Georgia on the state's 114,000 miles (183,465 km) of public roads and fifteen interstate highways. When President Dwight D. Eisenhower helped develop the national interstate system in the 1950s, Atlanta was chosen as the southeastern hub. The state's major highways are I-95 (which runs along the Georgia coast as it traverses from Maine to Florida), I-75 (which starts in Florida and passes through the northwestern corner of Georgia on its way to Michigan), and I-85 (which runs from Montgomery, Alabama, through Georgia, to Petersburg, Virginia). Other major highways in Georgia include I-20, I-575, and I-675.

Ports It may be hard to believe that a mostly landlocked state like Georgia has a thriving shipping business. Yet Savannah is home to one of the busiest ports in the country. It handles about 80 percent of the cargo that arrives in Georgia by ship. Brunswick is the state's second-biggest port. Georgia also has several smaller ports along its rivers.

Georgia Industries

Today, Georgia is home to some of the biggest companies in the world. Twelve of the companies on the *Fortune* magazine list of the five hundred largest U.S. corporations have their headquarters in the state, including Coca-Cola and Home Depot. Hundreds of other Fortune 500 companies have offices or factories in the state.

Coca-Cola is one of the best-known Georgia products. The soft-drink giant began as a simple headache remedy created in 1886 by pharmacist Dr. John Stith Pemberton. It has gone on to become one of the most popular soft-drink companies in the world, with 450 different brands sold in 200 countries.

Georgia Business Booms

When Georgia's economy struggled after the Civil War, one newspaperman tried to give it a boost. Henry W. Grady was managing editor of the *Atlanta Constitution*. In the 1880s, he invented the phrase "New South." By promoting Georgia as a new, modern city, Grady was able to interest businesses from the North enough to invest millions of dollars in Georgia.

The Georgia economy got another boost in the 1960s, with help from Ivan Allen Jr. His father, businessman Ivan Allen Sr., had attracted new businesses to the state back in the 1920s with the slogan "Forward Atlanta." As mayor of Atlanta from 1962 to 1950, Ivan Allen Jr. helped bring the Braves, Hawks, and Falcons sports teams to Atlanta. During his term, more than fifty new buildings were constructed, including the Memorial Arts Center and Atlanta Civic Center.

Georgia experienced yet another boom in the 1980s and 1990s. People poured into the state from around the country, attracted by the low cost of living and warm temperatures. The population jumped from 5.4 million in 1980 to more than 8 million in 2000.

Helping with the population boom was the Summer Olympics, which was held in Atlanta in July 1996. The Olympics drew more than ten thousand athletes and two million spectators to the city. Many buildings were constructed, including new dormitories at Georgia State University (which housed the athletes) and Centennial Olympic Stadium (which was converted to Turner Field and is now the home of the Atlanta Braves baseball team).

In 1967, Georgia native Truett Cathy started a chain of chicken restaurants at an Atlanta mall. Since then, Chick-fil-A has expanded to more than 1,340 restaurants around the country. The company's spokescows have made famous the slogan "Eat Mor Chikin."

Coca-Cola, based in Atlanta, is one of the world's leading soft-drink companies. One-and-a-half billion of its products are served each day around the world.

In 1979, businessmen Bernie Marcus and Arthur Blank opened the first Home Depot in Atlanta. The company is now the world's largest home improvement retail store chain and the second-biggest retailer in the United States.

Georgia-Pacific is one of the biggest producers of tissue, paper, and building products in the world. Based in Atlanta, it has more than three hundred offices around the world.

Georgia is also home to the self-proclaimed "carpet capital of the world." The city of Dalton produces more than 80 percent of the carpets made in the United States.

Chapter 5

PEOPLE FROM GEORGIA: PAST AND PRESENT

Georgia has been the birthplace of many renowned people. Poets, artists, musicians, writers, inventors, and even a president have called this state home. The following are just a sample of Georgia's most notable residents.

James Edward Oglethorpe (1696–1785) There would not have been a state of Georgia if James Edward Oglethorpe had not convinced King George II of England to grant a charter for the colony in 1732. Oglethorpe was born in London and served in Parliament. His life changed forever when he saw his friend Robert Castell get thrown into prison for debts and die there of smallpox. Oglethorpe set up the Georgia colony as a refuge for debtors. Although few debtors actually made it to Georgia, it grew into a successful state.

Signers of the Declaration of Independence Georgia's three representatives who signed the Declaration of Independence in Philadelphia in the summer of 1776 are as follows:

Button Gwinnett (1735–1777) He was a member of the English colonial legislature, but when the Americans fought for independence, he joined them. Gwinnett later served in the Georgia legislature. In 1777, he was killed in a duel with a political rival.

Lyman Hall (1724–1790) He was a doctor from Connecticut. He moved to Georgia and served as a representative to the Continental Congress, which governed the thirteen colonies during the American Revolution. In 1783, he was elected governor of Georgia.

George Walton (ca. 1750–1804) Walton was one of the most successful lawyers in the colony. At twenty-six years old, he was the youngest man to sign the Declaration of Independence. In 1779, he became governor of Georgia.

George Walton was one of three Georgia representatives to sign the Declaration of Independence.

Eli Whitney (1765–1825) In the late 1700s, cotton was the main crop in Georgia, but it was difficult to harvest. It took workers about ten hours to pull a single piece of cotton lint from the seeds around it. In 1793, an inventor named Eli Whitney built a machine that used rollers and metal teeth to separate the cotton fiber from the seeds. He called his invention the cotton gin ("gin" was short for "engine"). Whitney's machine could clean 50 pounds (23 kilograms) of cotton per day. The cotton gin wasn't good news for everyone, though. Some people said that Whitney's invention made cotton so

Martin Luther King Jr. *(center)* marched on Washington, D.C., for jobs and freedom in 1963. Born in Atlanta, King called for nonviolent direct action for civil rights.

profitable that it led to more slavery in Georgia because more workers were needed to grow and pick the cotton.

Martin Luther King Jr. (1929–1968) This young pastor of the Ebenezer Baptist Church in Atlanta became the face of the civil rights movement. His nonviolent protests helped African Americans earn the right to vote and have equal rights in the nation. On August 28, 1963, more than 250,000 people gathered in front of the Lincoln Memorial in Washington, D.C., to hear King give his "I have a dream"

34

Georgia Writers

Georgia has been home to some of the greatest writers of yesterday and today. Joel Chandler Harris, Margaret Mitchell, and Alice Walker are just a few of the celebrated authors from the state.

Joel Chandler Harris (1845–1908) When Joel Chandler Harris was a teenager, he was hired to work on a plantation near Eatonton, Georgia. While there, he loved listening to the slaves tell their folk stories. Harris eventually used those stories as the model for his Uncle Remus book series, which featured the misadventures of Brer Rabbit and Brer Fox.

Margaret Mitchell (1900–1949) In 1926, when writer Margaret Mitchell hurt her ankle and had to stay at home, she decided to start working on a novel about the Civil War in Georgia. Her book *Gone with the Wind* was published in 1936. It became one of the most popular novels of all time. Hollywood producer David O. Selznick made a movie based on Mitchell's book. It premiered at the Loew's Grand Theatre in Atlanta on December 15, 1939.

Alice Walker (1944–) Alice Walker, born in Eatonton, Georgia, was the child of former sharecroppers. Walker's intellect gave her entry to Spelman, a prominent college for black women in Atlanta, and later Sarah Lawrence College in New York. Her novel *The Color Purple* earned Walker a Pulitzer Prize for Fiction and a National Book Award in 1983. In 1985, Steven Spielberg and Quincy Jones made *The Color Purple* into a movie. Walker's novel was also adapted as a musical, which premiered on Broadway in 2005.

Alice Walker was inducted into the Georgia Writers' Hall of Fame at Emory University in Atlanta in 2001.

speech. At only thirty-five years old, he became the youngest person to win the Nobel Peace Prize. On April 4, 1968, King was shot and killed by James Earl Ray while standing on a balcony at the Lorraine Motel in Memphis, Tennessee. In honor of King's work, Congress established the third Monday in January as a national holiday—Martin Luther King Jr. Day. In the year of King's death, his widow, Coretta Scott King, established the King Center in Atlanta to preserve his legacy and promote his ideals of justice, equality, and peace.

Ray Charles (1930–2004) Charles lost his sight at age seven. He became a legend in the music world. He blended rhythm and blues, country, gospel, and jazz in such famous songs as "Hit the Road Jack" and "Georgia on My Mind." Charles was such a talented singer and musician that people called him "the Genius."

Jimmy Carter was not only elected a Georgia governor but also a U.S. president. Carter was president from 1977 to 1981.

Jimmy Carter (1924–) In 1976, this former peanut farmer from Plains, Georgia, was elected the thirty-ninth president of the United States and became the first president from Georgia. While he served as president, Carter led the Camp David agreement in 1978 that helped bring peace between Israel and Egypt. Since his presidency, Carter and his wife, Rosalynn, have worked with Habitat for Humanity, an organization that builds homes for people in need. In Atlanta, he founded the nonprofit Carter Center, which promotes human rights and democracy around the world. Carter was awarded the Nobel Peace Prize in 2002 for his human rights efforts.

Julia Roberts (1967–) This leading actress has appeared in the popular movies *Mystic Pizza* (1988), *Steel Magnolias* (1989), *Pretty Woman* (1990), *Oceans Eleven* (2000), and *Oceans Twelve* (2004), among others. She began her life in Smyrna, Georgia. In 2001, Julia Roberts won an Oscar for her title role in the movie *Erin Brockovich*. Six years later, *Forbes* magazine ranked her at number six on its list of the "20 Richest Women in Entertainment."

Timeline

1566	Spanish admiral Pedro Menéndez de Avilés explores the coast of Georgia.
1732	King George II grants a charter for the colony of Georgia.
1733	James Oglethorpe and 120 colonists arrive in Georgia.
1776	Three Georgians sign the Declaration of Independence.
1777	Georgia adopts its first state constitution.
1788	Georgia ratifies the U.S. Constitution, becoming the fourth state to enter the Union.
1793	Eli Whitney invents the cotton gin.
1838	The U.S. government forces the Cherokees to leave Georgia in the march now known as the Trail of Tears.
1845	Atlanta becomes a city (it is named the state capital in 1868).
1861	Georgia, with other southern states, secedes from the Union, beginning the Civil War.
1864	Union general William T. Sherman and his troops march into Atlanta.
1870	Georgia is readmitted to the Union.
1915	A boll weevil infestation destroys Georgia's cotton crops.
1964	Martin Luther King Jr. wins the Nobel Peace Prize.
1977	Jimmy Carter becomes the thirty-ninth president of the United States.
1996	Atlanta hosts the Summer Olympic Games.
2002	Former president and Georgia native Jimmy Carter wins the Nobel Peace Prize.
2003	A new state flag is created and approved by the Georgia General Assembly.
2007	A team from Warner Robins, Georgia, wins the baseball Little League World Series.

Georgia at a Glance

State motto	"Wisdom, justice, and moderation"
State capital	Atlanta
State flag	Three horizontal stripes of red and white, with a blue square in the upper-left corner, make up the flag. In the square is the state seal. Around the seal are thirteen white stars that symbolize the first U.S. colonies. This flag was adopted on May 8, 2003.
State seal	Three pillars support an arch on which is written the word "Constitution." The pillars symbolize the three branches of government. Each is wrapped in a scroll inscribed with a word from the Georgia state motto: "Wisdom, justice, and moderation."
State flower	Cherokee rose
State bird	Brown thrasher
State tree	Live oak
State vegetable	Vidalia onion
Statehood date and number	January 2, 1788; the fourth state
State nicknames	"The Peach State," "Goober State" (in honor of the peanut crop), "Empire State of the South"
Total area	57,906 square miles (149,976 sq km)
U.S. rank	Twenty-fourth-largest state

State Flag

State Seal

Approximate population at most recent census	9,363,941
Length of coastline	100 miles (160 km)
Highest and lowest elevation	Brasstown Bald, which is 4,784 feet (1,458 meters) above sea level; sea level, where Georgia meets the Atlantic Ocean in the east
Major rivers	Chattahoochee River, Savannah River, Suwannee River, Toccoa River
Major lakes	Lake Allatoona, Lake Burton, Lake Lanier, Lake Hartwell, Clarks Hill Lake
Hottest and coldest temperatures recorded	112 degrees Fahrenheit (45 degrees Celsius) on July 24, 1953, at Louisville; -17°F (-27°C) on January 27, 1940, at Civilian Conservation Corps Camp F-16 in northern Georgia
Origin of state name	Named after King George II of England, who granted James Oglethorpe a charter to start the new colony
Chief agricultural products	Poultry, cotton, peanuts, pecans
Major industries	Carpets/textiles, cola, airplanes/aerospace

State Bird

State Flower

GLOSSARY

amendment A change to a piece of legislation, such as a bill, law, or constitution.

basin A bowl-shaped area of land.

Confederate A person who supported the Southern Confederate states during the American Civil War.

constitution A written document that sets up the principles and laws for a government of a state or country.

desegregate To make a place accessible to people of all races.

discrimination Unequal or unlawful treatment based on race, color, religion, sex, or national origin.

gross domestic product (GDP) The total value of all goods and services produced in a state or country.

hydroelectric power Energy that is generated by flowing water.

legislature A group of elected individuals who make and change laws.

lynch To kill someone when that person has not been tried and convicted of a crime.

patriot Someone who loves his or her country. During the Revolutionary War, a patriot was someone who fought against England for the sake of America.

plateau A high, flat piece of land.

Pleistocene epoch The time period beginning about two million years ago and ending about ten thousand years ago.

ratify To sign and give consent to, such as approving a new constitution.

reservoir A body of water used to store water for the community's use.

secede To withdraw from.

secession The withdrawal of southern states from the Union in 1860.

segregation The act of keeping people of different races separate.

sharecropper A farmer who gives a portion of his crops to the landowner in exchange for a home and plot of land.

sit-in A form of nonviolent protest in which protesters sit in a particular place (such as a restaurant) and refuse to move.

smallpox A contagious and dangerous disease that causes blistery bumps to form on the skin.

swamp An area of land that is covered in shallow water.

Union The Northern states during the Civil War.

veto A vote against a bill or decision by a senior lawmaker, such as a governor or the president.

Georgia Council for the Arts

260 14th Street NW, Suite 401

Atlanta, GA 30318

(404) 685-2787

Web site: http://www.gaarts.org

This state agency provides money and support for music, art, dance, and theater in Georgia.

Georgia Music Hall of Fame

P.O. Box 870

Macon, GA 31202

(888) GA-ROCKS (427-6257)

Web site: http://www.georgiamusic.org

The Georgia Music Hall of Fame traces the history of music in the state. The Allman Brothers, Kenny Rogers, and Gladys Knight are just a few of the musical residents who are featured here.

Georgia Soil and Water Conservation Commission

4310 Lexington Road

Athens, GA 30603

(706) 542-3065

Web site: http://gaswcc.georgia.gov

This agency helps preserve and improve water and soil resources in the state.

Georgia Sports Hall of Fame

301 Cherry Street

Macon, GA 31208

(478) 752-1585

Web site: http://gshf.org

Georgia is home to many sports teams, both college and professional. This museum celebrates the state's most successful athletes.

Georgia Wildlife Federation

11600 Hazelbrand Road

Covington, GA 30014

(770) 787-7887

Web site: http://www.gwf.org

This organization of gardeners, hikers, and fishermen seeks to conserve Georgia's natural resources.

Stone Mountain Memorial Association

P.O. Box 689

Stone Mountain, GA 30086

(770) 498-5658

Web site: http://www.stonemountainpark.org

The Stone Mountain Memorial Association helps maintain and protect Georgia's best-known attraction.

Web Sites

Due to the changing nature of Internet links, Rosen Publishing has developed an online list of Web sites related to the subject of this book. This site is updated regularly. Please use this link to access the list:

http://www.rosenlinks.com/uspp/gapp

Davis, Marc, and Eric Gill. *The Georgia Colony* (Our Thirteen Colonies). Mankato, MN: Child's World, 2003.

Doak, Robin S. *Life in the Thirteen Colonies: Georgia*. New York, NY: Children's Press, 2004.

Doherty, Craig A., and Katherine M. Doherty. *Georgia* (The Thirteen Colonies). New York, NY: Chelsea House Publishers, 2005.

Gherman, Beverly. *Jimmy Carter* (Presidential Leaders). Minneapolis, MN: Twenty-First Century Books, 2004.

Harkins, Susan Sales, and William H. Harkins. *Georgia: The Debtors Colony* (Building America). Hockessin, DE: Mitchell Lane Publishers, 2007.

Heinrichs, Ann. *Georgia* (This Land Is Your Land). Minneapolis, MN: Compass Point Books, 2003.

Marsh, Carole. *Georgia Indians*. Peachtree City, GA: Gallopade International, 2004.

Prentzas, G. S. *Georgia* (America the Beautiful). New York, NY: Children's Press, 2008.

Sonneborn, Liz. *A Primary Source History of the Colony of Georgia* (Primary Sources of the Thirteen Colonies and the Lost Colony). New York, NY: Rosen Publishing Group, 2006.

Stechschulte, Pattie. *Georgia* (From Sea to Shining Sea). New York, NY: Children's Press, 2008.

BIBLIOGRAPHY

Atlanta Business Chronicle. "Georgia GDP Rises to $396.5 billion in 2007." June 6, 2008.
Retrieved November 3, 2008 (http://atlanta.bizjournals.com/atlanta/stories/
2008/06/02/daily101.html).

Coleman, Kenneth. *A History of Georgia.* Athens, GA: University of Georgia Press, 1991.

Georgia.gov. "History of Georgia's Capital Cities." Retrieved October 28, 2008 (http://
www.georgia.gov/00/article/0,2086,4802_4987_15252433,00.html).

Georgia Office of the Secretary of State. "Branches of Georgia Government." Retrieved
October 28, 2008 (http://sos.georgia.gov/archives/tours/html/branches_of_
government.html).

Georgia Power. "Georgia Information–2007: Executive Summary." Retrieved October 15,
2008 (http://www.georgiapower.com/grc/pdf/georgia/1execsummary.pdf).

Gerster, Patrick, and Nicholas Cords. *Myth and Southern History.* Champaign, IL:
University of Illinois Press, 1989.

Hartsfield-Jackson Atlanta International Airport. "Fact Sheet." Retrieved October 15,
2008 (http://www.atlanta-airport.com/Default.asp?url = sublevels/airport_info/
gmpage.htm).

Hepburn, Lawrence R., ed. *Contemporary Georgia.* Athens, GA: Carl Vinson Institute of
Government, University of Georgia, 1987.

Martin, Suzanne. *Awesome Almanac: Georgia.* Wadworth, WI: B & B Publishing,
Inc., 1996.

New Georgia Encyclopedia. "Geographic Regions of Georgia: Overview." Retrieved
October 18, 2008 (http://www.georgiaencyclopedia.org/nge/Article.jsp?path = /
LandResources/Geography&id = h-948).

New Georgia Encyclopedia. "James Edward Oglethorpe." Retrieved October 18, 2008
(http://www.georgiaencyclopedia.org/nge/Article.jsp?id = h-1058).

NobelPrize.org. "Martin Luther King, Jr." Retrieved November 8, 2008 (http://
nobelprize.org/nobel_prizes/peace/laureates/1964/king-bio.html).

Prentzas, G. S. *Georgia* (America the Beautiful). New York, NY: Children's Press, 2008.

Sullivan, Buddy. *Georgia: A State History.* Charleston, SC: Arcadia Publishing, 2003.

University of Georgia Museum of Natural History. "Physiographical Regions of Georgia."
Accessed October 18, 2008 (http://dromus.nhm.uga.edu/ ~ GMNH/gawildlife/
index.php?page = information/regions#AP).

U.S. Census Bureau. "State & County QuickFacts: Georgia." Retrieved October 15, 2008
(http://quickfacts.census.gov/qfd/states/13000.html).

U.S. Geological Survey. "Chattahoochee Riverway Project." Retrieved October 18, 2008 (http://ga2.er.usgs.gov/bacteria/chattfacts.cfm).

Watson, Stephanie, and Lisa Wojna. *Weird, Wacky and Wild: Georgia Trivia*. Alberta, Canada: Blue Bike Books, 2008.

INDEX

A

AFLAC, 26
Atlanta Civic Center, 30
Atlanta Constitution, 30

B

boll weevils, 27, 28
Brown, James, 5

C

Carter, Jimmy, 5, 36–37
Charles, Ray, 5, 36
Chick-fil-A, 30
civil rights movement, 5, 18–19, 34
Civil War, 5, 16–17, 30, 35
CNN, 26
Coca-Cola, 5, 29
Confederate flag, 16

D

Delta Air Lines, 5, 27

G

Georgia
    and cotton farming, 26, 27, 28, 33–34
    economy, 5, 26–31
    famous residents, 5, 19, 32–37
    government, 20–25
    history, 5, 12–19, 32–34
    land/climate, 5, 6–11
    and peanut farming, 5, 26, 28, 36
    sports teams, 30
    and tourism, 8, 30
"Georgia on My Mind," 36
Georgia-Pacific, 31
Georgia State University, 30
gross domestic product, 26

H

Harris, Joel Chandler, 35
Hartsfield-Jackson Atlanta International
    Airport, 5, 26–27
Home Depot, 29, 31

I

Indian Removal Act, 15

J

Jim Crow, 18–19

K

King Jr., Martin Luther, 19, 34, 36
Ku Klux Klan, 18

M

Metropolitan Atlanta Rapid Transit
     Authority (MARTA), 28
Mitchell, Margaret, 35

O

Oglethorpe, James Edward, 13–14, 32
Okefenokee Swamp, 10, 11

P

Peach State, 26
Pemberton, John Stith, 29

R

Roberts, Julia, 37

S

segregation, 18–19
Spelman College, 35
Summer Olympics, 30

T

Trail of Tears, 15–16

U

United Parcel Service, 26
University of Georgia, 19

W

Walker, Alice, 5, 35
Whitney, Eli, 28, 33–34

About the Author

Stephanie Watson is a writer based in Atlanta, Georgia. She is a regular contributor to several online and print publications, and she has written or contributed to more than two dozen books, including *Weird, Wacky and Wild Georgia Trivia* (as coauthor).

Photo Credits

Cover (top left) © MPI/Getty Images; cover (top right) © Thomas S. England/Time-Life Pictures/Getty Images; cover (bottom) © www.istockphoto.com/Laura Young; pp. 3, 6, 12, 20, 26, 32, 38 Shutterstock.com; p. 4 (top) © GeoAtlas; pp. 7, 28 © AP Photos; p. 9 © www.istockphoto.com/Danny Orlando; p. 10 © Raymond Gehman/Corbis; p. 13 © Stock Montage/Getty Images; p. 15 © Superstock, Inc./Superstock; pp. 18, 36 © Hulton Archive/Getty Images; p. 19 © Bettmann/Corbis; p. 21 Georgia Archives; p. 22 © age footstock/Superstock; p. 24 © Georgia Senate; p. 27 © Jim Richardson/Corbis; p. 31 © Eric S. Lesser/Zuma Press; p. 33 © Kean Collection/Getty Images; p. 34 © Robert W. Kelley/Corbis; p. 35 © Peter Kramer/Getty Images; p. 39 (left) Courtesy of Robesus, Inc.; p. 39 (right) Georgia Senate; p. 40 Wikipedia.

Designer: Les Kanturek; Editor: Kathy Kuhtz Campbell;
Photo Researcher: Marty Levick